To Georges Lemaître, Belgian astronomer and physicist
—Pascal Lemaître

Special thanks to Dr. Elliott Horch, professor of physics at Southern Connecticut State University, whose expertise, careful attention, and invaluable help in reviewing this book are greatly appreciated.

WHAT ABOUT™

THE UNIVERSE

An Illustrated Q&A Book for Kids

By Bertrand Fichou
Illustrated by Pascal Lemaître

We're going to talk about the universe!

Stellar!

Twirl

WHAT DOES E=MC² MEAN?

WHAT'S IT LIKE ON BOARD THE INTERNATIONAL SPACE STATION?

WHO WAS THE FIRST TO GO TO SPACE?

WHY ARE PLANETS ROUND?

WHY IS THERE SOMETHING RATHER THAN NOTHING?

That's what German philosopher and scientist Gottfried Wilhelm Leibniz asked a long time ago, and a question like that can take lifetimes to answer. For centuries, astronomers and physicists have tried to discover the true nature of the world—to trace its history back as close as possible to its beginning. And although they still haven't answered "why," they know more and more about "how."

This book seeks to answer a few of the questions we all ask about the origin of stars, the formation of planets, the astronomical speed of light, and the total darkness of black holes (which aren't actually holes—did you know that?).

With simple explanations and Pascal Lemaître's exhilarating illustrations, we've tried to lift the veil on the often incredible reality of our universe in small, digestible chunks. Ready for this interstellar voyage? Buckle your seat belt, and hold on tight!

Bertrand Fichou,
Images Doc

CONTENTS

A LITTLE GLOSSARY OF SPACE

The universe is everything that exists.

That's huge!

ASTEROID: A piece of rock, metal, and ice that travels through space.

ASTROLOGIST: A person who believes that the positions of celestial bodies in the sky influence human personality traits and destiny.

ASTRONOMER: A scientist who uses their knowledge of lenses and mirrors, and all forms of light to observe celestial bodies using different kinds of telescopes.

ASTRONOMICAL UNIT (AU): A unit used to measure distances in the solar system. One AU is 93 million miles (150 million kilometers), or the average distance between Earth and the Sun.

ASTROPHYSICIST: A scientist who studies how the universe works and applies the laws of physics to explain its existence.

ATMOSPHERE: The layer of gases that surrounds a planet or star. The air in Earth's atmosphere is 78 percent nitrogen and 21 percent oxygen.

ATOM: The basic building block of matter, which can be in a solid, liquid, or gas form. Atoms can combine with each other to create different materials.

BIG BANG THEORY: An explanation that scientists use to show the creation of the universe.

CELESTIAL BODY: A natural object in the sky, such as a star, planet, or comet.

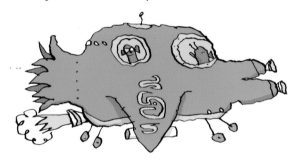

COMET: A frozen piece of dust, rock, and ice. When a comet orbits close to the Sun, it heats up and releases gases and dust, which form two tails: an ion gas tail and a dust tail.

COSMOS: Another word for "universe."

DENSITY/DENSE: The measurement of how much matter an object has compared with the space it takes up in volume. On Earth, an object that is denser than water sinks, while an object that is less dense than water floats.

ENERGY: What is needed to change an object's motion or move it around against a force (like gravity). Energy makes the stars and planets turn, and it also lets you stand upright or throw a ball.

EXOPLANET: A planet located outside our solar system.

GALAXY: A very large group of stars.

GENERAL RELATIVITY: The theory developed by Albert Einstein to explain the force of gravity through an understanding of the relationship between space and time.

GRAVITY: According to Isaac Newton, gravity is the force that draws two objects toward each other. It's what pulls you toward the center of Earth. According to Albert Einstein, objects create an attraction toward each other when they distort space around themselves.

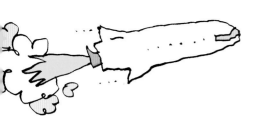

LIGHT-YEAR: The distance light travels in one year in the vacuum of space, or about 5.88 trillion miles (9.46 trillion kilometers).

MATTER: Everything that can be touched, or anything that takes up space. Mass is the measurement of how much matter there is.

METEOR: A piece of rock or metal from space that travels into Earth's atmosphere and burns up, creating a streak of light. The trail of light is the reason why we also call a meteor a shooting star.

METEORITE: A meteorite is a chunk of rock or metal from space that strikes the ground on Earth.

MILKY WAY: The name of our galaxy.

MOLECULE: A group of atoms bonded together.

NEBULA: An enormous cloud of gases and dust.

ORBIT: The set path of an object as it moves around a planet or star. The Moon orbits Earth, which orbits the Sun.

PARTICLE: An object smaller than an atom. There are many different kinds. Some particles form atoms, while others make up light.

STAR: A ball of gas that gives off light and heat.

SUPERNOVA: An extremely bright, powerful explosion that occurs when a massive star stops producing heat and energy.

PLANET: A celestial body that's large enough to be round, revolves around a star, and clears its orbital path of other objects.

SATELLITE: An object that orbits another. The Moon is Earth's only natural satellite, while the International Space Station is an artificial satellite orbiting Earth.

SPACE: The universe beyond our atmosphere.

SPACE-TIME: Albert Einstein describes the universe as a space-time, where space and time are linked. This theory states that the presence of matter distorts space and slows down time, and that nothing travels faster than light.

WEIGHTLESSNESS (OR ZERO GRAVITY): Weightlessness is when you can't feel any force, such as gravity, pulling on you. Astronauts aboard the International Space Station experience weightlessness. While gravity pulls the station toward Earth, the station's speed keeps it in a stable orbit. The astronauts aren't being pulled in either direction and feel like they're floating.

WHAT IS THE UNIVERSE?

This is a very simple question.

I'm suspicious of very simple questions.

THE UNIVERSE IS EVERYTHING

The universe is everything that exists: the Sun, Earth and the other planets that orbit it, the stars and the space between them. But the universe is also the time that goes by as you read these words, not to mention the energy that makes everything move, shine, and live.

THE UNIVERSE HAS A HORIZON

No one knows the shape of the universe because astronomers can't see farther than the cosmic horizon, which is about 45 billion light-years from us. That's *very* far away! Everything located between us and the cosmic horizon is called the observable universe.

THE UNIVERSE IS EXPANDING

The stars in the universe are growing farther apart the same way chocolate chips in cookie dough move when they're baking in the oven.

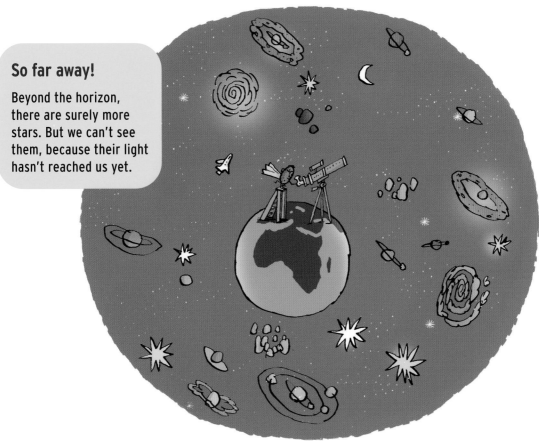

So far away!

Beyond the horizon, there are surely more stars. But we can't see them, because their light hasn't reached us yet.

WHAT'S AT THE END OF THE UNIVERSE?

No one knows! Some astronomers think that the universe is infinite, while others think that it's finite but has no edge, much like the surface of a ball: An ant could walk on the ball for its entire life without ever reaching an edge.

I'm on the edge of exhaustion!

If the universe is like a giant ball, what's around it?

There can't be anything around it, since the universe is EVERYTHING that exists. Anything around it would still be the universe!

Amazing!

The stars, the planets, light—everything we can observe makes up only a small part of the universe. The rest of the universe is mostly full of unknown forms of matter and energy called dark matter and dark energy. Astronomers can't see them, but they can measure their effects on the motions of stars and galaxies.

WHAT IS THE BIG BANG?

It's a way to describe the beginning of our universe.

Scientists' experiments and calculations all tell the same story. You'll see—it's amazing!

The universe was smaller than this!

A TINY UNIVERSE TO START!

About 13.8 billion years ago, the universe formed a sort of burning-hot soup where all the matter and energy in the world was mixed together. The universe was tiny, much smaller than the smallest speck of dust your eyes can see!

ALMOST LIKE AN EXPLOSION

Suddenly this "soup" started to swell up and inflate at an unimaginable speed. This moment, which we call the big bang, is often described as a gigantic explosion. No one knows what caused it.

An explosion usually explodes somewhere. However, when the universe started to expand, it didn't explode anywhere: Nothing else existed around it, and nothing else existed except it! No place existed outside the universe, not even a void or blackness. Nothing!

THE UNIVERSE CREATED SPACE... AND TIME!

It's very difficult to imagine: The universe wasn't born into an empty space—it created space and filled it. And what's harder to understand is that as it came into being, the universe also created time, because before the big bang, there was no past, present, or future!

If time didn't exist before the big bang, then does "before the big bang" mean anything?

Uh... you're trying to confuse me!

BIG BANG!

BIGGER AND BIGGER

Galaxies are very large groups of stars. They're moving away from each other. And the farther apart they get, the faster they go. The universe is expanding, like a balloon being inflated. So if the universe is growing, that means that it used to be much smaller.

Did you know?
The expression big bang was invented in the 1950s by English astronomer Fred Hoyle. He wanted to make fun of his colleagues who said the universe was expanding. He believed the universe was stationary, not growing.

Start the clock! Time has just been born, and we're off!

HOW ARE STARS BORN?

It's all thanks to gravity....

Grateful for gravitation!

1 A NEBULA DRIFTS THROUGH SPACE.

A nebula is an enormous cloud of gases and dust. Nebulas are found almost everywhere in the universe.

2 THE NEBULA SHRINKS.

The atoms that make up the gases and dust are drawn together by a force called gravity.

Little by little, they get so close that the nebula tightens up. It collapses in on itself.

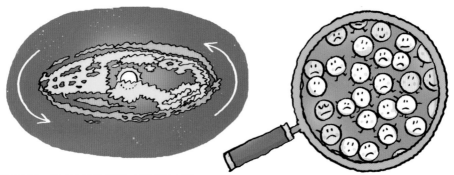

3 EVERYTHING STARTS TO HEAT UP.

The more the atoms of gases squeeze together, the more they jostle one another, increasing the amount of pressure. The greater the pressure, the more heat is created. It's similar to what happens when you use a bicycle pump: The more you compress the air, the hotter the pump feels in your hands.

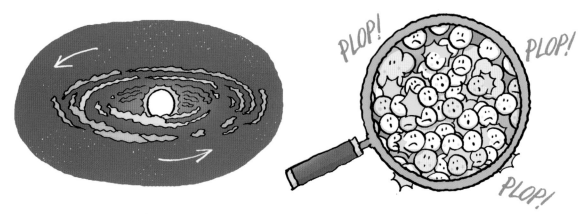

④ THE STAR IGNITES!

Inside the nebula, the heat and pressure force the atoms to stick to each other and create larger atoms. They fuse together, and this fusion produces energy, which escapes in the form of light and heat. The star begins to shine. Releasing the energy also prevents the star from shrinking.

⑤ PLANETS FORM AROUND THE STAR.

As the nebula collapses in on itself, it spins and flattens out like a plate. Some areas have more gases and dust than others. In the center, they cluster together to make a star. On the edges, they form planets that will orbit around the star.

Calabash Nebula, also known as Rotten Egg Nebula

What's in a name?

Some nebulas have interesting names, such as the Crab Nebula, the Butterfly Nebula, the Eagle Nebula, and the Cat's Eye Nebula. But the Rotten Egg Nebula makes you wonder what it smells like!

WHY DOES THE MOON REVOLVE AROUND EARTH?

To be more accurate, we should say "Why does the Moon FALL around Earth?"

Oh really? What do you mean?

IMAGINE WHAT HAPPENS . . .

1 When you kick a rock, it goes up. But because of the force of gravity, it's attracted to Earth and falls back to the ground.

2 If you throw the rock, it will go higher and farther than it did the first time, but it will still end up falling back to the ground.

3 Say you're superstrong and you throw your rock really hard. It will go even higher and farther, and it will fall back down. But . . .

4 If the rock goes very far up, it will never fall back to the ground. It will start orbiting Earth the same way that the Moon does.

SO WHO "THREW" THE MOON?

1 No one! It all happened more than 4 billion years ago, when a huge rock came from outer space and collided with one side of Earth.

2 The impact tore chunks of rock out of our planet and tossed them into space. Because of gravity, these rocks began to revolve around Earth.

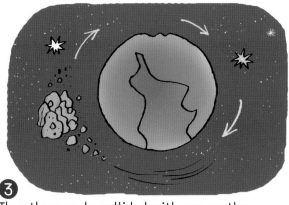

3 Then these rocks collided with one another, fused together, and eventually formed a ball that became our Moon!

Did you know?

In space, an object that revolves around another is called a satellite. Earth has only one natural satellite, the Moon, but thousands of artificial satellites. Since the launch of the first satellite in 1957, thousands more have been sent into space. These satellites transmit radio, TV, and cell phone signals, and provide information about the weather, climate, and many other things.

It's taking my picture!

James Webb Space Telescope

Hubble Space Telescope

Looking back further

One of the most famous satellites is the Hubble Space Telescope, which was launched in 1990 to gather information about the stars, planets, and galaxies. Its light-collecting mirror measures almost 8 feet (2.4 meters) in diameter. It was joined in 2021 by the more powerful James Webb Space Telescope, which has a mirror that is over 21 feet (6.5 meters) in diameter and will provide even more precise images of the universe.

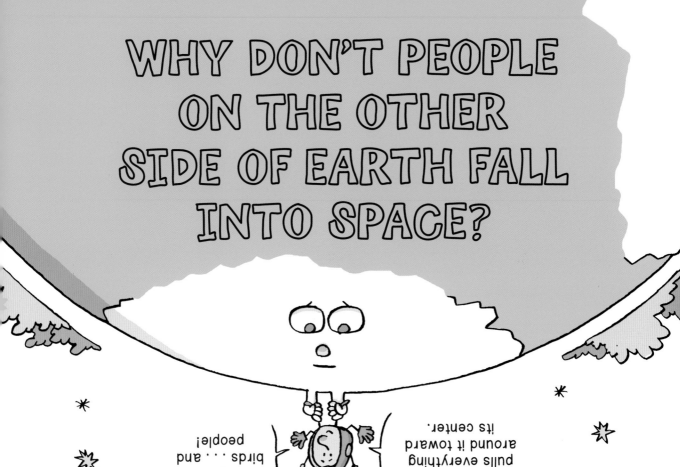

WHY DON'T PEOPLE ON THE OTHER SIDE OF EARTH FALL INTO SPACE?

It's because Earth pulls everything around it toward its center.

Rocks, water, birds . . . and people!

EARTH PULLS ON US

Everyone on the planet keeps their feet on the ground because Earth's gravity pulls them toward its center. Gravity is also the reason why a rock you throw into the air falls back to the ground. And it is also why it's tiring to climb a flight of stairs.

GRAVITY RULES THE UNIVERSE

In the universe, all objects attract each other. The force trying to bring them together is called gravity. The bigger the objects are, the more they attract each other. And the closer they are together, the more they attract each other.

WATCH YOUR HEAD!

It was Isaac Newton who laid out the law of universal gravitation. It's said that he got this idea from watching an apple fall to the ground. Some even say the apple fell on his head, but that's a myth!

Round and round
You may feel like you're walking on the top of Earth, and people on the other side are at the bottom. But Earth really has no top or bottom. It has an almost completely round shape, so its surface is curved.

ARE SHOOTING STARS REALLY STARS?

No. A shooting star is a space rock that burns up as it enters Earth's atmosphere.

Most of these rocks are actually the size of a grain of sand. They're also called meteors.

MOVING MOLECULES

Our planet is surrounded by a layer of several different gases called the atmosphere. Gas is made up of invisible molecules that move freely, are constantly in motion, and collide with one another.

SPEEDY ROCKS

Small rocks in space are called meteoroids. A rock that enters the atmosphere, called a meteor, travels fast, at about 43 miles (70 kilometers) per second. When it collides with the gas molecules, it heats up (the same way your hands warm up when you rub them together). As the meteor burns, we see the light that it emits. That's what we call a shooting star.

WATCH OUT!

Most meteors completely burn up in the sky and become part of the atmosphere. Some don't completely burn up, and those that fall to Earth are called meteorites. The Hoba meteorite is the largest that has ever been found on Earth. Weighing about 119,000 pounds (54,000 kilograms), it was discovered in Namibia in 1920.

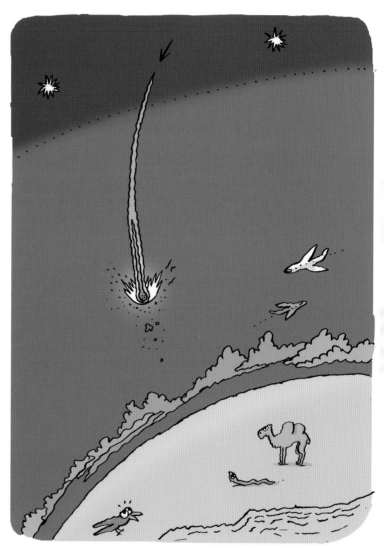

Did you know?

On February 15, 2013, rocks rained down on the city of Chelyabinsk in Russia. They were pieces of a meteoroid more than 65 feet (20 meters) wide that exploded as it entered Earth's atmosphere.

IS IT TRUE THAT STARS ARE ATTRACTED TO EACH

That's what astronomers have seen through their telescopes.

But it seems there are two different explanations. . . .

ACCORDING TO ISAAC NEWTON

Planets and stars attract each other because of gravity. Newton noticed that the bigger and closer they are, the more attracted to each other they are. But because there is a lot of empty space between stars and planets, gravity doesn't always cause them to collide or orbit each other.

Did you know I'm attracted to you?

Sorry, but I'm more attracted to my big orange friend here!

1 For Newton, the closer the blue planet gets to the yellow star, the more the two bodies are attracted to each other because of gravity.

2 As the fast-moving planet gets close, its path curves toward the star. However, the planet eventually continues on its set path and moves away from the star.

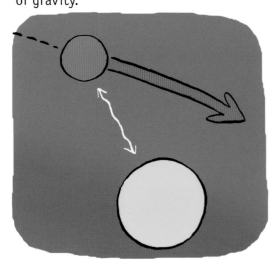

AND PLANETS OTHER?

ACCORDING TO ALBERT EINSTEIN

Albert Einstein thought that planets and stars deform, or change the shape and size, of space around them. The more matter that these planets and stars contain, the more they change space. Einstein believed that gravity isn't a force, but an effect produced by space as it deforms.

Imagine the celestial bodies are two marbles on a trampoline.

The blue planet approaches the yellow star....

1 For Einstein, the yellow star, which is very big, curves space around it. It deforms space.

2 The blue planet continues on its path, but the deformation of space pulls the planet off its original straight-line path.

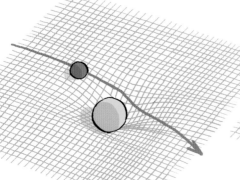

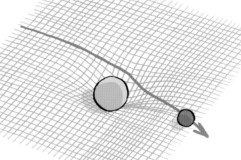

Two theories

Newton's and Einstein's explanations both describe the movements of stars in the universe very well. They allow us to calculate their paths very precisely.

Who's more right? Einstein or Newton?

Einstein, until someone comes up with an even better explanation.

WHY DO PEOPLE SAY WE'RE MADE OF STARDUST?

Well, the astronomer Carl Sagan once said, "We're made of star stuff."

And some people call that stardust!

Recipe for a person →

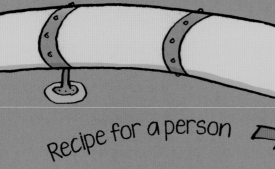

YOUR BODY IS MADE OF ATOMS

Atoms can be imagined as microscopic marbles that make up all the matter in the world—everything we can touch. Even our bodies are made of atoms.

Okay, I'm made of billions of atoms. But where do they come from?

MOST ATOMS WERE MADE INSIDE STARS

When the universe began, there were only little atoms of hydrogen (one of the chemical elements that make up water) and helium (the gas used to blow up birthday balloons). Hydrogen and helium formed the first stars. As they burned, the stars transformed them into bigger and more complex atoms of hydrogen and helium.

Mix

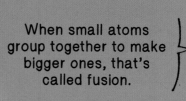

When small atoms group together to make bigger ones, that's called fusion.

STARS DIE AND DISPERSE THEIR ATOMS

When stars die, many of them explode and disperse the atoms they made into outer space. These atoms group together elsewhere, forming clouds or nebulas, which give birth to new stars. In each new star, the atoms burn and gather to create bigger and more varied atoms. And planets will eventually appear around the stars.

That's how our solar system, Earth, and living things came to be!

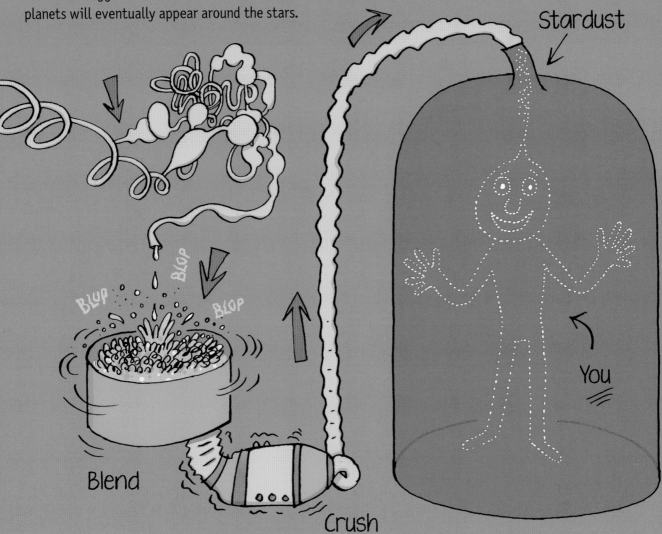

Stardust

Blend

Crush

You

SO YOUR BODY IS MADE OF "STAR STUFF"!

The calcium in your bones and the iron that makes your blood red were made by stars that disappeared billions of years ago!

This is mind-boggling!

Nothing is lost, nothing is created, everything is transformed.

ANTOINE LAVOISIER, French chemist

CAN YOU TIME TRAVEL?

Yes, but not the way they do in movies.

WHAT IF YOU MET CLEOPATRA?

Human beings have long dreamed of inventing a machine to travel back into the past or forward into the future. Can you imagine meeting Cleopatra in ancient Egypt or your future grandkids? Well, that's impossible right now!

Hello! I'm selling high-performance vacuum cleaners!

40 BCE

LOOKING INTO THE DISTANCE IS LOOKING INTO THE PAST

What *is* possible is "seeing" the past. When you look at a star, its light is reaching you after a long trip through space. You're seeing the star as it was when its light left it, which means you're seeing far into the past! You can even see stars that no longer exist—they burned out while their light was traveling toward Earth.

THE SUN AND THE MOON

Light travels at a speed of 186,000 miles (300,000 kilometers) per second. Since the Sun is 93 million miles (150 million kilometers) away from Earth, its light takes 8 minutes to reach us. So you're seeing the Sun as it was 8 minutes ago! The Moon is 239,000 miles (384,000 kilometers) from Earth, so its light (which is a reflection of the Sun's light) takes 1.3 seconds to reach us. This means we see the Moon as it was a little more than 1 second ago!

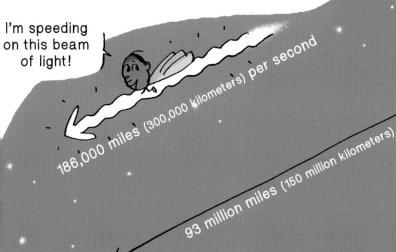

I'm speeding on this beam of light!

186,000 miles (300,000 kilometers) per second

93 million miles (150 million kilometers)

239,000 miles (384,000 kilometers)

A TELESCOPIC JOURNEY!

The star closest to our own is called Proxima Centauri. It's located four light-years away, which means that its light traveled for four years to reach us. We're seeing that star as it was four years ago. And thanks to telescopes, scientists can see it really well.

Amazing!

The James Webb Space Telescope was launched on December 25, 2021. It will be able to see stars being born more than 13 billion years ago!

What would happen . . .

It might be fun to think about traveling to the past, but it could actually create impossible situations. We call them paradoxes. For example: Someone travels to the past to stop an event from happening, but in the course of doing this, one of their ancestors dies in an accident. This means that the time-traveler wouldn't have been born, so they couldn't travel back in time to stop the event.

Hello, future Grandpa!

HOW MANY STARS ARE THERE IN THE SKY?

I would say a lot!

It really depends on how well you see.

AN ASTRONOMICAL NUMBER

Astronomers think that the observable universe contains around one hundred thousand billion billion stars, or 100,000,000,000,000,000,000,000 of them, which is a "1" followed by 23 zeroes. You can also write: 10^{23} stars. That's quite a lot!

1000000000

WHAT IF WE COUNTED GRAINS OF SAND?

Our galaxy, called the Milky Way, "only" contains 200 billion stars. That's about how many grains of sand it would take to fill the back of a small van.

WITH THE NAKED EYE

At night, if you look at the sky when there are no clouds and there's a clear view of the horizon, you'll be able to make out about 3,000 stars. And you would see about the same number if you were on the other side of Earth, so 6,000 in total. That's a pretty big number!

Amazing!

At night, your eyes see better from the side than right in the middle. Try an experiment: Pick a star, stare at it, then look a little to one side. . . . It's surprising, right?

IS IT COLD IN OUTER SPACE?

 Well, let's say it's very hot *and* very cold.... What kind of an answer is that?

THE UNIVERSE IS VERY COLD . . .

The prevailing temperature way out in space, far from stars and planets, is −454°F (−270°C). That's c-c-c-cold! In comparison, water in your refrigerator freezes at 32°F (0°C), and the coldest temperature on Earth was recorded at around −130°F (−90°C) in Antarctica.

. . . BUT IT CAN ALSO BE VERY HOT!

Astronauts on the surface of the Moon must wear protective spacesuits. When they face the Sun, they are exposed to a temperature of 260°F (127°C). In the shade, temperatures are −173°F (−280°C)!

On Earth, the atmosphere disperses the heat of the Sun in all directions. An ice cream cone exposed to the Sun will melt faster than one in the shade, but the temperature difference isn't more than 36°F (2°C).

Did you know?
Absolute zero is the extremely cold temperature at which atoms and molecules are at their lowest energy point and stop moving. It is zero on the Kelvin scale, equivalent to -459.67°F (-273.15°C).

BRRR ... IT'S FREEZING OUT HERE!

WHY IS ALBERT EINSTEIN SO FAMOUS?

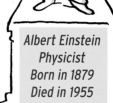

He worked out the theory of general relativity.

And we haven't seen the world the same way ever since!

Albert Einstein
Physicist
Born in 1879
Died in 1955

GENERAL RELATIVITY

Einstein believed that planets and stars (and everything that exists) move through what he called space-time. Space and time are linked, and all objects distort space and time around them. For example, a planet changes the course of the celestial bodies near it. Even light changes course when it passes close to a star. And time flows at different speeds, depending on where you are. It sounds unbelievable, but for a hundred years, scientists have been conducting experiments that prove that Einstein was right!

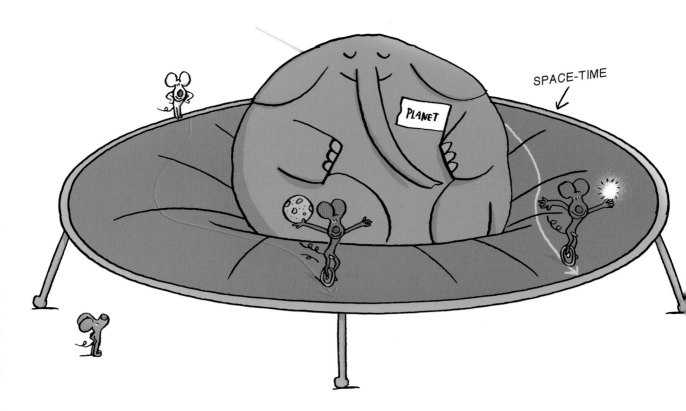

PLANET

SPACE-TIME

EINSTEIN'S DISCOVERIES INCLUDE:

TIME ISN'T THE SAME FOR EVERYONE

The closer you are to a massive object, the slower time passes. For example, a clock placed at the bottom of a staircase advances more slowly than the same clock placed at the top of the same staircase. The first is closer to the center of Earth than the other, so time moves more slowly for it!

THE FASTER YOU GO, THE MORE TIME SLOWS DOWN

If we only consider the motion of a plane and not the effects that Earth's gravity has on it, then the hands of a clock traveling on the plane will appear to turn more slowly to an observer who is not moving and who has an identical clock on the ground. If the clock on the plane is brought to the clock on the ground and the two are compared side by side, the plane's clock will indeed be slow! These differences are very slight, and we don't feel them in our daily lives. But if Einstein hadn't discovered that time is relative, GPS would be much less precise: GPS uses satellites that correct these time variations.

LIGHT HOLDS THE RECORD FOR SPEED

In a vacuum, nothing moves faster than light, at a speed of 186,000 miles (300,000 kilometers) per second. And light travels at the same speed everywhere in the universe.

WHAT DOES E=MC² MEAN?

It's the most famous mathematical formula in the world!

It was set forth by the physicist Albert Einstein to describe our universe.

THE ENERGY OF MATTER

To understand this formula, you have to know that everything you can touch (a table, a tree, a cat, your body, and so forth) is made of matter. And matter is made of atoms, which are made up of even smaller particles. These particles are stuck together by mysterious forces.

Everything is swarming with tiny particles!

WHAT IS THIS FORMULA?

In a mathematical formula, each letter or symbol means something specific.

So E=mc² says the energy in an object equals its mass multiplied by the speed of light squared.

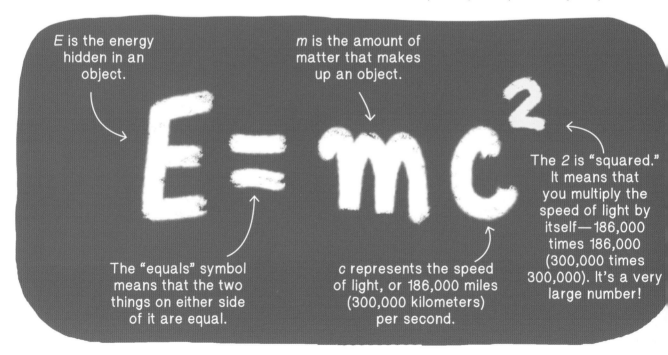

E is the energy hidden in an object.

m is the amount of matter that makes up an object.

$$E = mc^2$$

The 2 is "squared." It means that you multiply the speed of light by itself—186,000 times 186,000 (300,000 times 300,000). It's a very large number!

The "equals" symbol means that the two things on either side of it are equal.

c represents the speed of light, or 186,000 miles (300,000 kilometers) per second.

THE SENTENCE THAT EXPLAINS THE WORLD!

$E=mc^2$ means that matter in our universe contains lots of energy. And that matter can be transformed into energy, and even that energy can become matter.

For example: In a star, hydrogen is converted into helium, in a process called fusion. Just a small amount of the star's matter produces a huge amount of energy. This energy produces light and heat.

Using machines called particle accelerators, scientists speed up the movement of particles, which are inside atoms. The movement energy that is generated allows the scientists to create matter.

WHO WAS THE FIRST TO GO TO SPACE?

Leaving Earth took a lot of courage.

No one knew if we could survive the flight.

FLIES!

The first spaceflight was made by . . . fruit flies! They were launched in 1947 by the U.S. aboard a V-2 rocket. After reaching an altitude of 68 miles (109 kilometers), their capsule returned to Earth by parachute. They were still alive.

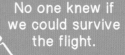

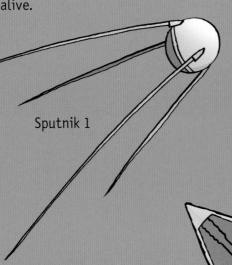

Sputnik 1

THE FIRST OBJECT IN ORBIT

The first piece of equipment that humans succeeded in placing into orbit was a Russian satellite named Sputnik 1. This ball of metal, the size of a large beach ball, started going around Earth on October 4, 1957. It marked the beginning of the space race.

DOGS, CATS, AND MORE

The first living thing put into orbit was a dog named Laika. Russia launched her aboard Sputnik 2 on November 3, 1957, but, unfortunately, she did not survive. Other animals flew later, including Félicette the cat, turtles, worms, and even bacteria.

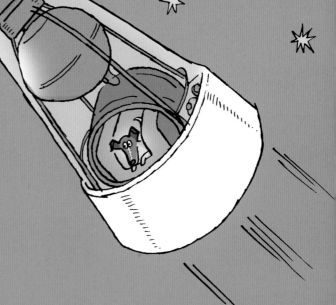

THE VERY FIRST PERSON

The very first person to go into space in a rocket was Russian cosmonaut Yuri Gagarin. On April 12, 1961, he took off on board the Vostok 1 spacecraft. He went once around Earth in a 108-minute flight that reached an altitude of 203 miles (327 kilometers). It was an extraordinary event!

Breaking News!
First in Space!

THE FIRST WOMAN

In 1963, Russian cosmonaut Valentina Tereshkova became the first woman in space. She orbited Earth 48 times on board the Vostok 6 spacecraft, a flight that lasted almost three days.

Did you know?

Not all people who go into space are called astronauts. The term used depends on where they're from. The Russians are known as cosmonauts. The French are spationauts. The Chinese are taikonauts.

WHAT'S IT LIKE ON BOARD THE INTERNATIONAL SPACE STATION?

The International Space Station is longer than a football field!

But with only six players, it's hard to have a game.

LIVING IN SPACE

The International Space Station (ISS) measures 357 feet (109 meters) from one end to the other. It is designed for six astronauts to live and work in air-filled modules that are shaped like canisters. Most astronauts live there for three to six months.

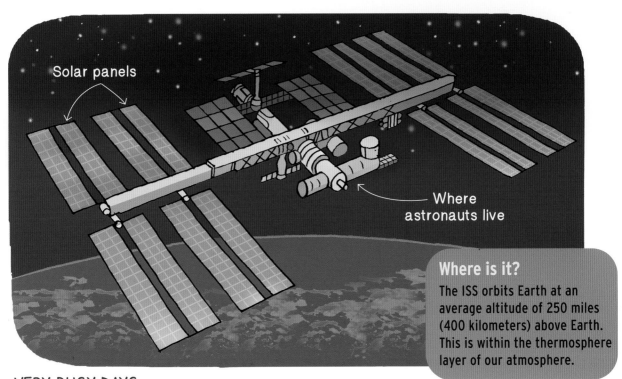

Solar panels

Where astronauts live

Where is it?

The ISS orbits Earth at an average altitude of 250 miles (400 kilometers) above Earth. This is within the thermosphere layer of our atmosphere.

VERY BUSY DAYS

On board the ISS, the astronauts have many tasks. They clean and check out equipment, fix broken parts, test clocks to improve the GPS, conduct experiments to understand how human bodies react to weightlessness, grow plants, exercise, and much more.

EVERYTHING FLOATS!

On board the ISS, there's no up or down, and everything that isn't held in place simply floats around. Watch out for drops of water and crumbs that could damage the equipment!
- The astronauts don't take baths. They wash with wet wipes.
- The toilets suck up poop, and the astronauts pee into tubes.
- They sleep in sleeping bags fastened to the walls.
- They drink soup and soda from packets using straws.
- In the weightless environment, human bodies have less resistance and work differently than they do on Earth. To stay fit and prevent bone loss and weakened muscles, astronauts have to work out for at least two hours a day.

WATCH OUT FOR RADIATION!

In outer space, the astronauts are exposed to as much radiation in one day as they would be in a year on Earth! That can cause diseases. Scientists have to figure out how to protect people from this much radiation before long, multiyear voyages are planned.

SPACE IS LITTERED WITH TRASH

The ISS often encounters debris from spacecraft and micrometeorites. Some pass by at 12 miles (20 kilometers) per second; at that speed, a 0.5 inch (1 centimeter) piece of gravel can pierce a module! Two escape vessels are attached to the space station to return the astronauts to Earth in case of an emergency.

Did you know?

Peggy Whitson holds the record for the most time spent in space—665 days! She was also the first female commander of the ISS. There, she conducted many experiments and made 10 spacewalks to install and repair equipment. After retiring from NASA in 2018, she joined Axiom, a private spaceflight company. "It never gets old, looking at the curve of the Earth," she said in 2021.

HOW FAST DO ROCKETS GO?

To reach orbit around Earth, rockets have to take off at more than 17,000 miles (28,000 kilometers) per hour, or they will fall back down.

Some go even faster!

SUPER SPEEDY

The rocket that carried the New Horizons probe toward Pluto in 2006 took off from Earth at the fastest speed, clocking 36,400 miles (58,536 kilometers) per hour.

The fastest object built by humans is the Parker Solar probe, which reached a speed of 364,660 miles (586,864 kilometers) per hour. It has come within 3.83 million miles (6.16 million kilometers) of the Sun's surface. That's the closest a spacecraft has ever been to the Sun!

The International Space Station moves at a speed of 17,500 miles (28,000 kilometers) per hour. Traveling at this speed means that the ISS goes around Earth every 90 minutes. The crew on board experiences 16 sunrises and sunsets in one day!

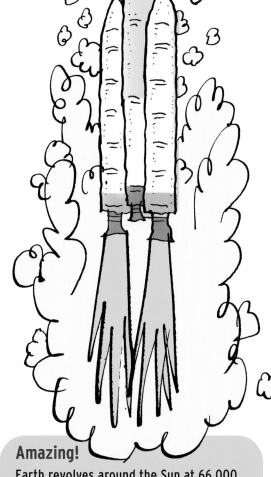

Amazing!

Earth revolves around the Sun at 66,000 miles (106,000 kilometers) per hour as it spins on its own axis. So, in a way, you're spinning, too! If you live in North America, you reach a speed of 671 miles (1,080 kilometers) per hour, without moving a muscle or even realizing it!

Did you know?

Most Apollo spaceflights have taken a little more than three days to reach the Moon. How long it took depended on where the Moon was in its orbit around Earth when the rocket launched. It also depended on the size of the spacecraft and the type of fuel used.

HOW LONG DOES IT TAKE TO GET TO MARS?

Going to the Moon and back can take about a week.

A trip to Mars would take much longer than that! At the moment, we aren't ready to send people there.

NOT A DAY AT THE BEACH!

Living on Mars won't be easy. Because it is farther from the Sun, it is colder than Earth. The average temperature is −81°F (−63°C)! Sandstorms sweep the whole planet and block out the Sun, sometimes for months.

Welcome, earthlings!

A LARGE SPACECRAFT

The spacecraft will need to be big enough to carry six astronauts, along with oxygen, water, and food. It will also need to have very heavy shielding to protect against cosmic radiation. The amount of fuel required for the long journey will take up half the weight of the ship!

Hello, Earth?

40 minutes later . . .

Message delays
A message transmitted from Mars would take 5 to 20 minutes to reach Earth. This means that there would be a time lapse of 6 to 40 minutes between a message and its reply!

ONE DEPARTURE EVERY TWO YEARS

Every two years, Mars and Earth are at their closest to each other, 34 million miles (55 million kilometers) apart. With today's technology, a crewed spacecraft would take 200 days to reach Mars. It would have to stay there for 500 days, then take another 200 days to come back to Earth. That's at least two and a half years of adventure!

Hello, who is this?

WILL HUMANS LIVE ON MARS ONE DAY?

We would have to terraform Mars first!

Hmm . . . changing the red planet into a blue planet. Well, why not?

YEAR ZERO

100 YEARS

200 YEARS

A FAR-FETCHED IDEA

Before settling on Mars, we'd have to already be able to travel there and back safely. In theory, this idea doesn't seem completely impossible, but for now, robots are the ones sent to explore the planet.

WE WOULD NEED *LIQUID* WATER . . .

There's lots of ice on Mars. It covers the poles and is hidden under the soil. People would have to transform the frozen water into liquid water. To do that, Mars would need to be heated up, which can be done by increasing the thickness of its atmosphere. That can be achieved by freeing carbon dioxide trapped in the soil.

Did you know?

On Mars, the atmospheric pressure is weak. That means that the atmosphere is very thin, so things don't weigh much on the planet's surface. Because of that, water boils at 50°F (10°C), while on Earth it boils at 212°F (100°C).

. . . AS WELL AS OXYGEN

In the water and carbon dioxide of Mars, there's oxygen, the same gas that we breathe in our air. So people could make the atmosphere of Mars breathable by using machines to extract the oxygen from the water and carbon dioxide. We could also grow algae and lichens, which give off oxygen.

Eat your veggies!
If plants could be grown on Mars, they would be a main source of food for its inhabitants. People would need to eat plant-based meals because it would be much too complicated, and less nourishing, to raise animals there.

600 YEARS

900 YEARS

1,000 YEARS

IT WOULD TAKE AT LEAST 1,000 YEARS

Martian residents would grow mosses, which are "oxygen factories." It would take about 700 years before the mosses release enough oxygen to grow the first flowering plants, then bushes, and finally pine forests. In a thousand years, they could grow tomatoes.

What an idea!
Some scientists have thought of placing giant mirrors in orbit above the poles on Mars, believing that these mirrors would reflect the light of the Sun and melt the ice. The mirrors would be 155 miles (250 kilometers) wide.

43

WHY ARE PLANETS ROUND?

Yes! Why aren't they square?

Or flat like pancakes?

GRAVITY LOVES CURVES

Planets are round because of gravity. A planet forms when rocks and dust in outer space are drawn toward each other. They group together, and gravity forces them all toward the place where they're already the most numerous, which is the center.

At first, it is a dance.

VISCOUS BALLS

When a planet forms and it's at least 310 miles (500 kilometers) wide, the rocks inside it press so hard against each other that they heat up and melt. The planet becomes a mass of liquid lava that, because of gravity, eventually becomes more ball-shaped.

I feel dizzy!

NOT ENTIRELY ROUND

But planets are never completely round. They spin, so they're a little wider at the equator and flattened at the poles because of centrifugal force. You might have felt this force if you spin around and let your arms relax. Your arms will extend away from your body, similar to the expansion of a planet's midsection.

I love to spin and don't want to stop!

WHY ALL ROCKS AREN'T ROUND

A rock measuring less than 310 miles (500 kilometers) wide doesn't contain enough matter for gravity to change its shape.

I'll need a lot more rocks to become nice and round!

IS TRAVEL TO JUPITER POSSIBLE?

It is, but there's a catch: There is no ground to land on!

THREE KINDS OF PLANETS

In our solar system, there are three types of planets:

- Rocky planets have a solid surface made of rock and are closest to the Sun. They are Mercury, Venus, Earth, and Mars.
- Gas giants are much bigger than the rocky planets and are mostly made of hydrogen and helium. The two gas giants are Jupiter and Saturn.
- Ice giants are much farther from the Sun and are colder planets that are made of elements heavier than hydrogen and helium. These planets are Uranus and Neptune.

Amazing!

Earth is a rocky planet. Its exterior crust is a solid layer of rock 3 to 50 miles (5 to 80 kilometers) thick. But Earth's interior is made of various layers that are more or less liquid and paste-like.

Oh, no!

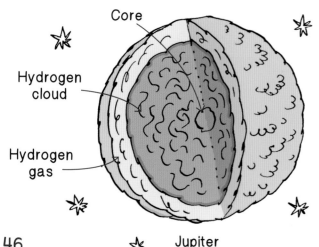

Core

Hydrogen cloud

Hydrogen gas

Jupiter

WHAT WOULD HAPPEN IF WE WENT TO JUPITER?

A spacecraft that approached Jupiter would first disappear into its clouds, then encounter fierce storms and winds of more than 370 miles (600 kilometers) per hour! Very quickly, the clouds would block light from the Sun, and it would be completely dark.

A ONE-WAY TRIP

Deep inside Jupiter, the clouds are wetter, thicker, and hotter, eventually becoming a burning, liquid ocean. Even deeper, hydrogen transforms into a molten metallic state, and the core is a metallic ball. However, the spacecraft would have vanished well before reaching the center, crushed by the weight of the atmosphere!

Did you know?

Jupiter is the biggest planet in the solar system. It is 1,300 times larger than Earth, and its center is three times hotter than the surface of the Sun!

WHAT IS A COMET?

For a long time, people believed they were signs from the gods.

But they didn't know whether they were good signs!

COSMIC SNOWBALLS

A comet is a frozen piece of dust, rock, and ice that orbits the Sun. As it passes close to the Sun, ice in the comet heats up and releases gases and dust, forming a cloud around the nucleus called a coma, as well as two tails.

Amazing!

Comets contain lots of frozen water. It resembles ocean water on Earth. Some scientists think that much of the water found on Earth came from comets.

HOW BIG IS A COMET?

Most comets have a center that is no more than 6 miles (10 kilometers) wide. But the tails of some comets can be 100 million miles (160 million kilometers) long!

HALLEY'S COMET

More than 4,500 comets currently orbit our Sun. The most famous is Halley's Comet. Its body measures 9 miles (15 kilometers) wide, and it can be seen in our sky, on average, every 76 years. It will appear over Earth again in 2061!

Did you know?

In 2014, a spacecraft succeeded in landing a small probe called Philae on a comet passing close to Jupiter. The trip took ten years! Philae was able to send back to Earth the first photos from the surface of a comet.

WHAT WILL HAPPEN TO EARTH IN THE FUTURE?

 A long time from now, it may not exist.

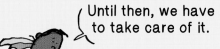 Until then, we have to take care of it.

THE SUN MIGHT SWALLOW EARTH

The Sun and Earth have existed for 4.5 billion years. They're about halfway through their life span. When the Sun burns up all the hydrogen in its core, it will swell up and swallow the planets around it: Mercury, Venus, and possibly even Earth. Our planet will get very hot, oceans will evaporate, and all life will disappear from its surface. But that will not happen for about 5 billion more years.

WHAT CAN WE DO?

To avoid the end of Earth? Nothing. By that time, our descendants will likely have discovered how to build spacecraft to colonize planets in other solar systems.

THE REAL DANGER ISN'T EARTH DISAPPEARING

Humans are damaging our planet so quickly that it might become uninhabitable within a few hundred years. For future generations to live here for a long time, we have to:
- Limit global warming, which causes sea levels to rise and enlarges desert areas.

- Preserve biodiversity. Biodiversity is the large number of animal and plant species that live in different regions of our planet. The extinction of any species has lasting effects on its ecosystem.

WHAT IS THE MILKY WAY?

The Milky Way is the name of our galaxy.

WE SEE IT IN THE SKY

If you observe the sky carefully on a moonless night, you'll see a wide band of whitish light above you. That's the Milky Way. Our solar system is part of it.

WHAT IS A GALAXY?

A galaxy is a group of many, many stars surrounded by gases and dust. Some galaxies, like our Milky Way, form what look like giant wheels that spin. Our galaxy contains around 200 billion stars!

THE CENTER OF OUR GALAXY

If you look at the sky in the direction of the constellation Sagittarius*, you're looking in the direction of the center of the Milky Way. But you won't be able to make out this region with the naked eye, because it's hidden by enormous clouds of dust.

*To orient yourself, check out the maps of the sky on pages 72–75.

DIFFERENT SHAPES

The observable universe contains several hundred billion galaxies. Some are elliptical (they look like footballs), while others form spirals or are irregularly shaped. The Milky Way is a spiral galaxy.

Elliptical galaxy

Barred spiral galaxy

Irregular galaxy

Did you know?

The Milky Way measures 100,000 light-years** wide. That means that if a star lights up on the edge of the Milky Way, an observer positioned on the other side will see its light arrive 100,000 years later!

Amazing!

If the observable universe were the size of a soccer field, our Milky Way would be a tiny grain of sand in the middle.

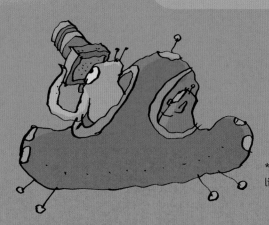

**Find out more about light-years on page 56.

51

WHAT'S IN OUR

Astronomers say there are eight planets in our solar system.

That depends on what you call a planet. . . .

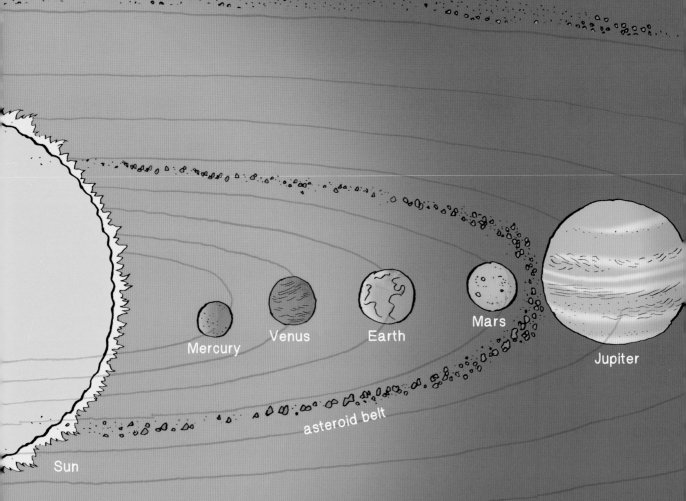

Sun

Mercury

Venus

Earth

Mars

Jupiter

asteroid belt

NOT JUST THE EIGHT PLANETS

Eight planets orbit our Sun, and they carry with them 175 natural satellites. There are also five dwarf planets and billions of pieces of rocks, comets, and asteroids. The Sun and all the celestial bodies that orbit it form what we call the solar system.

SOLAR SYSTEM?

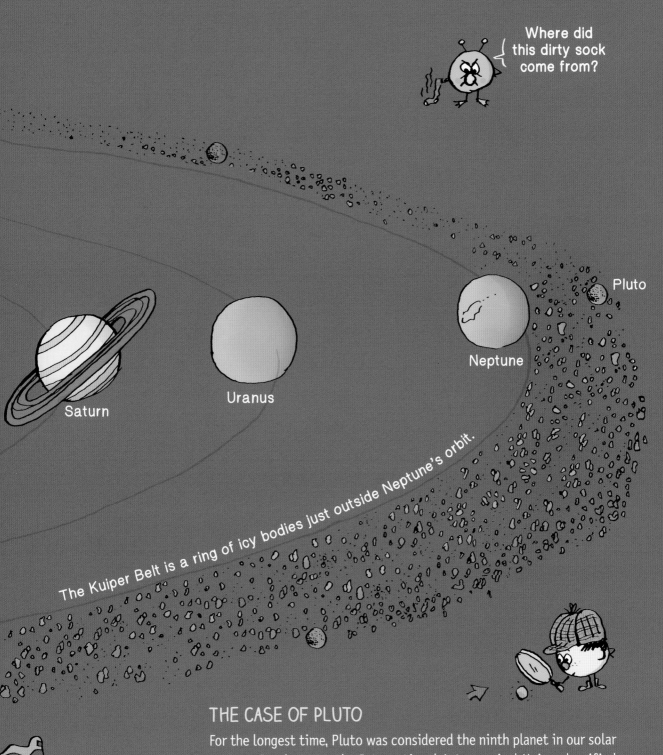

Where did this dirty sock come from?

Pluto

Neptune

Saturn

Uranus

The Kuiper Belt is a ring of icy bodies just outside Neptune's orbit.

The Kuiper Belt

THE CASE OF PLUTO

For the longest time, Pluto was considered the ninth planet in our solar system. But in 2006, the International Astronomical Union classified Pluto as a dwarf planet when it more specifically defined what a planet is. As a small celestial body 1,473 miles (2,370 kilometers) across— smaller than our Moon—Pluto could not fulfill one of the rules, which is that a planet needs to have a clear path in its orbit around the Sun. It is now the most famous object in the Kuiper Belt!

WHAT'S THE DIFFERENCE BETWEEN ASTRONOMY AND ASTROLOGY?

Astronomy is a science.

 Astrology is a belief.

ASTROLOGISTS

Astrologists are interested in the position of the planets in the sky. They believe that these celestial bodies shape our personalities and influence what happens in our lives. Different forms of astrology have been practiced by various cultures since ancient times. The most familiar form is sun sign astrology, based on the 12 signs of the zodiac.

ASTRONOMERS

Astronomers are scientists. They try to understand how the universe formed and how it works. By observing through telescopes, they can calculate the path of planets, analyze the light from the stars to find out what they're made of, and try to discover how the universe will develop.

Mercury must be in retrograde!

Is it real?

Lots of people believe in astrologers' predictions because they need to feel reassured and to make sense of what's happening around them. While it may be entertaining to talk about, it is unlikely that the stars and planets have any influence over people's behavior, or their future.

I was born under a lucky star!

WHAT ARE EXOPLANETS?

Extraterrestrials have to live somewhere!

Where do *you* live?

SEARCHING FOR EXOPLANETS

If extraterrestrials exist, perhaps they live on other planets that orbit stars similar to our Sun. These planets are called exoplanets.

Exoplanets are very far away, and they're hard to spot because the stars that they orbit around are so bright. Astronomers can detect them using telescopes: The gravity of the exoplanets changes their stars' movements, and the light of the stars dims when the exoplanets pass in front of them.

NOT ALL ARE HABITABLE

Astronomers have spotted thousands of exoplanets, but not all of them can support living things. They think that for life to develop, there has to be liquid water, which means a planet must be neither too close to nor too far from its star, and it has to have an atmosphere.

At the moment, scientists have found fewer than 100 habitable exoplanets. However, in our galaxy alone, there could be around 500 million!

WILL WE EVER TRAVEL AT THE SPEED OF LIGHT?

That would be nice. Stars aren't exactly next door!

But we won't get to enjoy the view. . . .

LIGHT IS MIND-BLOWING!

Across the universe, light always moves at the same speed—186,000 miles (300,000 kilometers) per second. This means that in just 1 second, light can go around Earth 7.5 times!

WHAT'S A LIGHT-YEAR?

In outer space, the distances are so large that we don't measure them in miles or kilometers, but in light-years. A light-year is the distance light travels in one year, or about 5.88 trillion miles (9.46 trillion kilometers). That's an extremely huge number!

IMPOSSIBLE . . . FOR NOW!

It's difficult to imagine that we might someday travel at the speed of light. Albert Einstein calculated that in order to go that fast, we would have to use an infinite amount of energy. And we don't know how to do that yet!

> **Did you know?**
> When you turn on a lamp, you think that the light appears the exact moment you flip the switch. In reality, it has to cross the distance between the bulb and your eye, and that takes a little bit of time. But it's too fast for you to notice it.

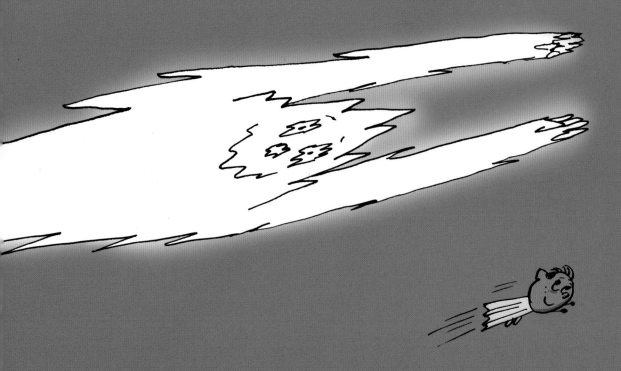

SO FAR AWAY

Proxima Centauri is the star closest to our Sun. It's located four light-years away from us, and the Voyager 1 interstellar probe would take 80,000 years to reach it!

The Moon is about one light-second from Earth, or 239,000 miles (384,000 kilometers) away, which is a small distance in the big picture of the whole universe.

The stars on the other side of the Milky Way orbit 70,000 light-years away from us. Our telescopes see them as they were in the time of the Neanderthals.

The Sun is 8 light-minutes, or about 93 million miles (150 million kilometers), from Earth.

The Orion Nebula, visible to the naked eye, is 1,500 light-years from us. That means we see it as it was at the beginning of the Middle Ages.

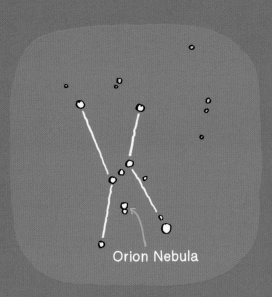

Orion Nebula

HOW BIG IS THE SUN?

If the Sun was the size of a pumpkin . . . . . . Earth would be the size of a pea. And they would be 295 feet (90 meters) away from each other.

IT'S HUGE

The Sun measures about 865,000 miles (almost 1.4 million kilometers) wide. You could line up 109 Earths across the face of the Sun, or fit 1.3 million Earths inside it!

IT WILL BURN FOR BILLIONS MORE YEARS

The hydrogen in the core of the Sun is fused into helium at a great temperature and pressure to produce light. The amount of helium produced per second is equivalent to what 800 giant oil tankers can carry! But it's so big that it will continue to produce heat and light for billions more years.

Even bigger!

The star Antares, which you can see in the Scorpius constellation, is 900 times bigger than the Sun. And the largest known star is called UY Scuti. It's 1,700 times bigger than the Sun!

Did you know?

Eruptions can be observed on the surface of the Sun. They don't spew out lava like volcanoes, but particles. When these particles reach Earth, they disrupt our systems of communication and produce auroras, bands of colored light that appear in the skies above the North and South Poles.

WHAT IS A CONSTELLATION?

It's like a connect-the-dots puzzle.

An imaginary drawing in the sky!

GIANT DRAWINGS

A constellation links together several stars, as well as the area that surrounds the drawing. There are 88 of them covering our whole sky like an enormous puzzle.

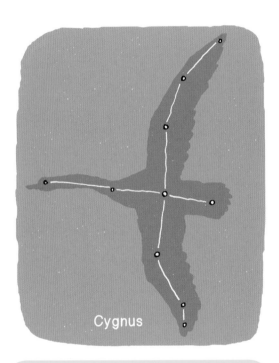

Cygnus

Shape-shifters

Because stars travel through space, the shapes of the constellations change over time. For example, during prehistoric times, the Big Dipper didn't have the same shape it does today.

STORIES IN THE SKY

In the ancient world, humans oriented themselves on Earth by looking at the position of the stars. They grouped them together so they'd be easier to "read." They drew animals and heroes from their legends in the sky, and told stories about them.

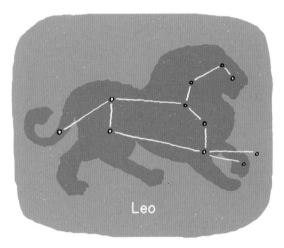

Leo

HEROES, ANIMALS, OBJECTS

The modern names of the constellations represent legendary heroes, such as Orion, Perseus, and Hercules; animals, such as Ursa Major (Great Bear), Cetus (Whale), and Canis Major (Great Dog); imaginary animals, such as Monoceros (Unicorn) and Phoenix; objects, such as Microscopium (Microscope) and Norma (Ruler); and people, such as Auriga (Charioteer) and Pictor (Painter).

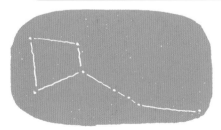

Big Dipper 10,000 years ago

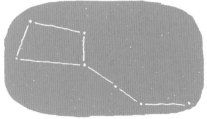

Big Dipper today

Big Dipper 10,000 years from now

HOW DO PLANETS AND STARS GET THEIR NAMES?

If I were in charge, I would name them after family members.

So there could be a Grandma Star!

Alcor

Mizar

Alkaid

THE PLANETS BEAR THE NAMES OF ROMAN GODS

In ancient times, the planets were visible to the naked eye, and people wondered what the lights in the sky could be. Thinking that perhaps they were gods, they decided to call them Mercury, Venus, and Jupiter, after the gods of the ancient Romans. Phobos and Deimos, the two moons of Mars, bear the names of Greek gods.

LOTS OF STARS HAVE ARABIC NAMES

Arab astronomers in the Middle Ages were meticulous and dedicated in their study of the stars. They lived in dry regions where the sky was often very clear, and they could observe the stars all year. They named the stars in the Big Dipper: Alkaid, Mizar, Alcor, Alioth, Megrez, Dubhe, Merak, and Phecda.

It's this way!

WHAT'S THE NAME?

While Mizar was given the name by Arab astronomers, the star is also known by other names, such as Zeta Ursae Majoris, Vasishta in traditional Indian astronomy, and the Lu star to Chinese astronomers.

Doctor, I don't know who I am anymore: Mizar, Zeta, or Lu?

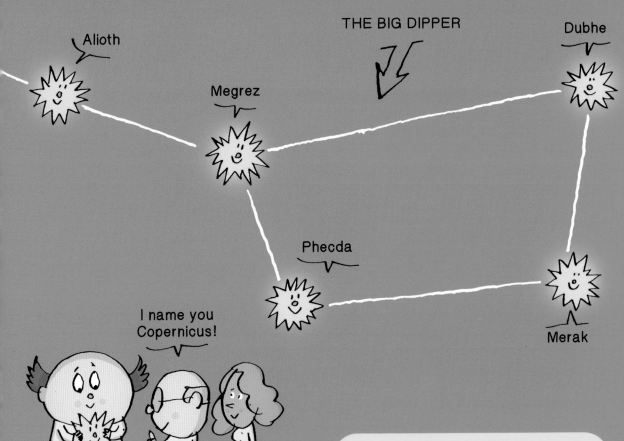

THE BIG DIPPER

Alioth

Megrez

Dubhe

Phecda

Merak

I name you Copernicus!

A NAMING SYSTEM

Today, the International Astronomical Union (IAU) gives stars and planets their names. The IAU is an association of astronomers from all over the world. It established guidelines on naming newly discovered stars and exoplanets.

Did you know?

Before GPS, Arab caravanners learned to find their way through the desert by looking at the position of the stars in the sky.

CAN YOU FALL INTO A BLACK HOLE?

No, because a black hole isn't an actual hole.

But if you get too close, you will have a bad time!

HOW DOES A BLACK HOLE FORM?

Imagine a star dying out. Under the effect of gravity, the star shrivels up or collapses in on itself. It takes up less and less space, but it's still made of the same amount of matter, like a chunk of bread you squeeze in your hand. If the star is big enough, it can eventually become what we call a black hole.

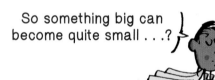

So something big can become quite small . . .?

WE CAN'T SEE IT

A black hole is a place in the universe where the matter is VERY dense, or very firmly packed. This ball of matter deforms space and attracts everything that comes close to it: stars, planets . . . even light! Nothing can escape black holes. That's why they can't be seen.

Telltale signs

If we can't see black holes, how do we know they exist? Well, we can detect them because they disrupt the movement of the stars around them.

It's like observing wind movement from behind a window. You can't feel or see the wind, but you know it's there because the leaves on the trees are moving.

CAN AN ASTEROID DESTROY EARTH?

Yes, but we won't let it happen!

I'm not afraid!

A QUESTION OF SIZE

Billions of asteroids orbit the solar system. When objects less than 16 feet (5 meters) wide enter Earth's atmosphere, they explode at a high altitude and don't do any damage. But an object much larger could devastate an entire region, and an asteroid 3 miles (5 kilometers) wide could wipe out human life! But we would see it coming from far away and take action before it got close to our planet.

ASTEROID DRILL

In November 2021, NASA launched an automated spacecraft to try to divert an asteroid from its path by crashing into it. The Double Asteroid Redirection Test (DART) is scheduled to crash into the space rock in late 2022. This should have the same effect as shooting a balloon with an arrow! The mission will allow for any revisions to the plan before we have to face a real danger.

THE END OF THE DINOSAURS

Non-avian dinosaurs went extinct 66 million years ago when an asteroid 6 miles (10 kilometers) wide hit Earth, causing worldwide destruction. The impact of the asteroid, which landed off what is now the Yucatán Peninsula in Mexico, stirred up a thick layer of dust and ash that blocked the Sun for more than two years. Most of Earth's plant and animal species also died out.

Did you know?

In 1908, a meteorite destroyed a Siberian forest within a 12-mile (20-kilometer) radius of the impact site, even though it exploded before reaching the ground. The blast was heard more than 900 miles (1,500 kilometers) away!

HOW DO WE KNOW WHAT WE KNOW ABOUT THE UNIVERSE?

We don't know everything, but that means there's more to discover!

THE LANGUAGE OF THE UNIVERSE

To study the universe, scientists learned to decipher its language: light! Light is a type of energy that travels in waves. Some waves are stronger and some are weaker, depending on where they fall on the electromagnetic spectrum. Our eyes can't detect all types of light, but scientists have invented special telescopes to see them. By studying these light waves, astronomers now know what type of matter makes up a distant star, or how fast it's moving away from us.

VISIBLE LIGHT

The colors that we can see—violet, indigo, blue, green, yellow, orange, red—or visible light, make up a small part of the electromagnetic spectrum. Violet has the shortest wavelength of all visible light, while red has the longest. Early astronomers observed the stars and planets using visible light, at first with the naked eye, then with telescopes.

Light with longer wavelengths have less energy. Light with shorter wavelengths have more energy.

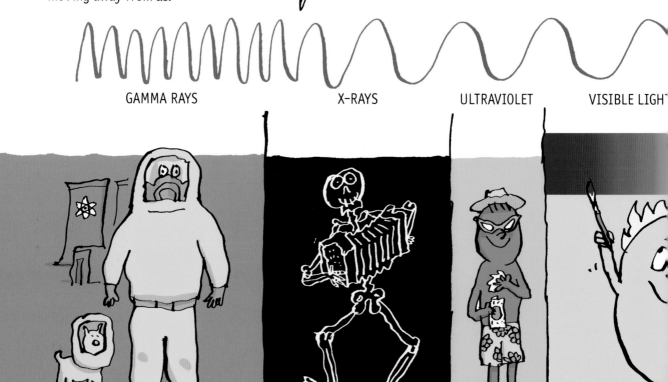

GAMMA RAYS   X-RAYS   ULTRAVIOLET   VISIBLE LIGH

Did you know?
While astronomers observe the enormous universe, physicists study the particles, the grains of matter or energy that fill the universe. And the more they study microscopic objects, the more they need huge machines! The world's largest and most powerful particle accelerator, the Large Hadron Collider (LHC), was installed in a loop-shaped tunnel more than 16 miles (27 kilometers) long, on the border between Switzerland and France. There are plans to build an even bigger accelerator: The tunnel for the Future Circular Collider would be 62 miles (100 kilometers) long!

"INVISIBLE" WAVES

Light that has a wavelength shorter than violet or longer than red make up invisible light. Light waves with less energy, or longer wavelengths, are infrared waves and, if they're stretched further, then radio waves. Light waves with more energy, or shorter wavelengths, become ultraviolet waves, then X-rays and gamma rays, which can travel through the human body. These two types of light are used in hospitals to take X-rays and other images.

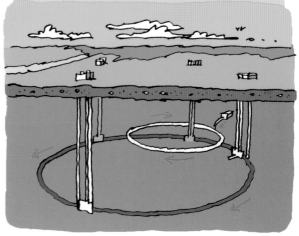

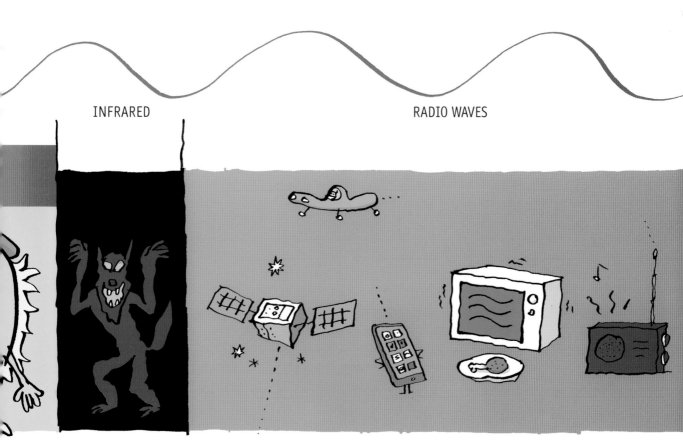

INFRARED

RADIO WAVES

ARE THERE OCEANS ON OTHER PLANETS?

Yes! Superdeep oceans.

Scientists wonder if they might even contain living things.

MORE WATER THAN EARTH

In our solar system, Earth is the only planet with oceans. Almost 75 percent of its surface is covered by them, which is why Earth is called the blue planet. However, several moons of Jupiter and Saturn have much larger oceans.

Did you know?

If Earth were a smooth ball, it would be covered by a layer of water 1.7 miles (2.7 kilometers) deep. It's a lot if you want to reach the bottom, but it's not much when compared with other oceans in the solar system.

THE BIGGEST OCEANS

Ganymede and Titan are moons of Jupiter and Saturn. Both are around 15 times smaller than Earth, but Titan may have 15 times more water than Earth, and Ganymede may have as much as 30 times more water than Earth. Because Ganymede and Titan are very far from the Sun, their oceans are under really thick crusts of ice.

If this is Earth . . .

. . . then this marble represents all the water on it.

And these are other celestial bodies in the solar system, with all the water on them. Impressive, isn't it?

celestial bodies

water

Enceladus   Dione   Europa   Pluto   Triton   Callisto   Titan   Ganymede

DEEP OCEANS

Ganymede has an enormous ocean of salt water that might shelter life-forms. Astronomers think that it's 62 miles (100 kilometers) deep. In comparison, the deepest place on Earth is in the Pacific Ocean, and it's less than 7 miles (11 kilometers) deep.

Geysers

The Cassini probe took photos of geysers bursting through the surface of Enceladus, a small moon of Saturn. If there are geysers, then that would mean that there's liquid water below the ice.

A CHANCE TO FIND LIFE

The ocean of Europa, another moon of Jupiter, is probably about 60 miles (100 kilometers) deep. Covered by an ice shelf, this water likely contains chemical elements rather similar to the ones in Earth's oceans. To study these oceans, scientists will have to send probes able to pierce through the extremely thick ice.

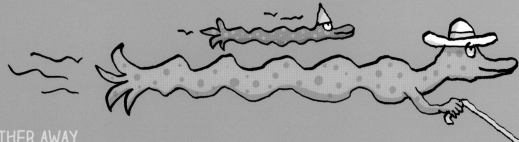

AND FARTHER AWAY

Astronomers have discovered the planet Proxima Centauri b outside our solar system. It may be a little larger than Earth, and it orbits the star Proxima Centauri. It's at the right distance from its star to have liquid water (it's not too hot or too cold), and it could have a surface with an ocean not covered by ice! It might even harbor life. In our galaxy, it is likely that thousands of distant planets have seas and oceans.

WHO ARE SOME STARS OF ASTRONOMY?

ERATOSTHENES
(circa 276 BCE/circa 194 BCE) **Greek**

He was the first to calculate the size of Earth.

CLAUDIUS PTOLEMY
(circa 100 CE/circa 170 CE) **Egyptian** of Greek descent

He believed that Earth was the center of the world. The Moon, the Sun, the planets, and the stars orbited around it. The stars were stuck to a sphere that marked the end of the universe.

GAN DE
(circa 400 BCE/circa 340 BCE) **Chinese**

He is believed to be one of the first people to compile a star catalog. His detailed observations of Jupiter and other planets, as well as his study of sunspots across the Sun, have been of valuable help to astronomers.

ARYABHATA
(476 CE/550 CE) **Indian**

He discovered that the stars appear to move westward because of Earth's rotation around its own axis. He also noted that the Moon and planets shine because they reflect the Sun's light.

TYCHO BRAHE
(1546 CE/1601 CE) **Danish**

With the assistance of the king of Denmark, he built Uraniborg, a very large observatory. He drew up a catalog of almost 800 stars.

NICOLAUS COPERNICUS
(1473 CE/1543 CE) **Polish**

He proposed that the Sun was the center of the world, and that Earth and the planets orbited around it.

GALILEO GALILEI
(1564 CE/1642 CE) **Italian**

He was the first to use a telescope to observe the sky. He discovered mountains on the Moon and the satellites of Jupiter.

WHO ARE SOME MORE STARS OF ASTRONOMY?

JOHANNES KEPLER
(1571 CE/1630 CE) **German**

With the help of Tycho Brahe's calculations, he discovered the laws that govern the movement of the planets. They don't go around in circles; they follow a somewhat oval path called an ellipse.

ISAAC NEWTON
(1642 CE/1727 CE) **English**

He invented the reflecting telescope, which uses mirrors and is more powerful than the refracting telescope, which uses lenses. He established the law of universal gravitation.

ANNIE JUMP CANNON
(1863 CE/1941 CE) **American**

She created the Harvard system of classifying stars. At Harvard College Observatory, she classified 350,000 stars—more than anyone else has done—and discovered five novas, and 300 variable stars, which are stars that change brightness.

HENRIETTA SWAN LEAVITT
(1868 CE/1921 CE) **American**

She discovered 2,400 variable stars and found a way to determine the distances between Earth and the galaxies based on the brightness of stars and how they change over time.

ALBERT EINSTEIN
(1879 CE/1955 CE) **German** and **American**

He developed the theory of general relativity, which is still the best description of the universe today.

EDWIN HUBBLE
(1889 CE/1953 CE) **American**

He discovered that galaxies are moving away from each other, which led to the big bang theory.

VERA RUBIN
(1928 CE/2016 CE) **American**

She proved the existence of dark matter through her studies of the movement of spiral galaxies. The Vera C. Rubin Observatory in Chile will open in 2023.

What's the white streak among the stars?

That's the Milky Way, our galaxy!

THE SKY SPINS!

Or rather, Earth spins, but to us, it looks as if the stars are moving. So, depending on the season, day, and hour, we don't see the same thing. We group stars into constellations, which bear the names of animals, objects, or legendary characters. You'll find them on this map.

Here's a tip

To observe the stars well, choose a moonless night. And get away from lights coming from streets and houses. At first, you'll see only the brightest stars; let your eyes adjust to the darkness for at least eight minutes.

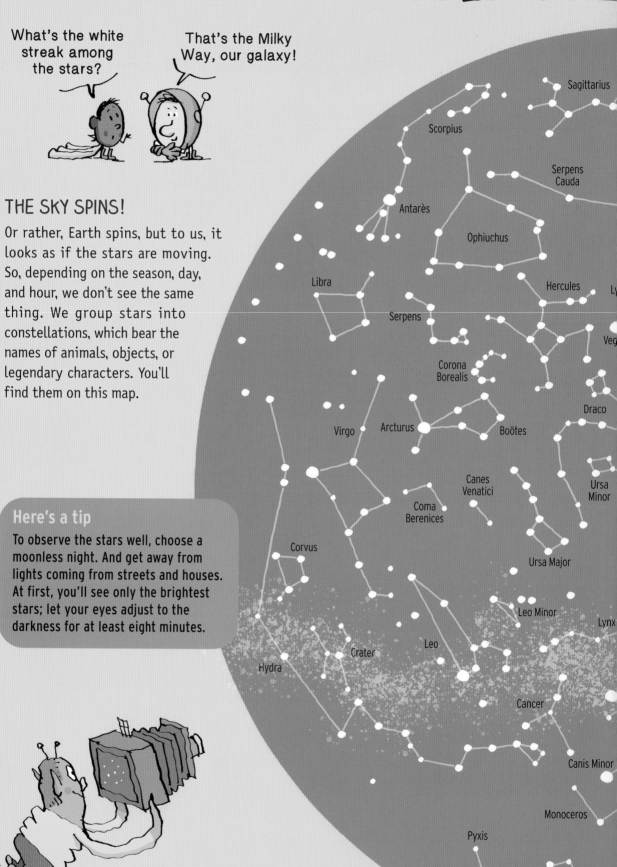

Sagittarius

Scorpius

Serpens Cauda

Antarès

Ophiuchus

Libra

Hercules

Ly

Serpens

Veg

Corona Borealis

Virgo

Arcturus

Boötes

Draco

Canes Venatici

Ursa Minor

Coma Berenices

Corvus

Ursa Major

Leo Minor

Lynx

Crater

Leo

Hydra

Cancer

Canis Minor

Monoceros

Pyxis

Puppis

This map shows stars and constellations you can see in the Northern Hemisphere. But you won't see them all at the same time.

NORTHERN NIGHT SKY?

THE MOST VISIBLE CONSTELLATIONS

All year, you can easily recognize Cassiopeia with its M or W shape, and the Big Dipper in the shape of a saucepan. Right in the middle between Cassiopeia and the Big Dipper, you'll find a lone star: the famous North Star. Its location above Earth's North Pole makes it seem as if the sky turns around it.

In the winter, the Orion region is very recognizable above the southern horizon. From Orion, you can easily find Taurus, as well as Auriga the Charioteer, with Capella and its three little goat stars.

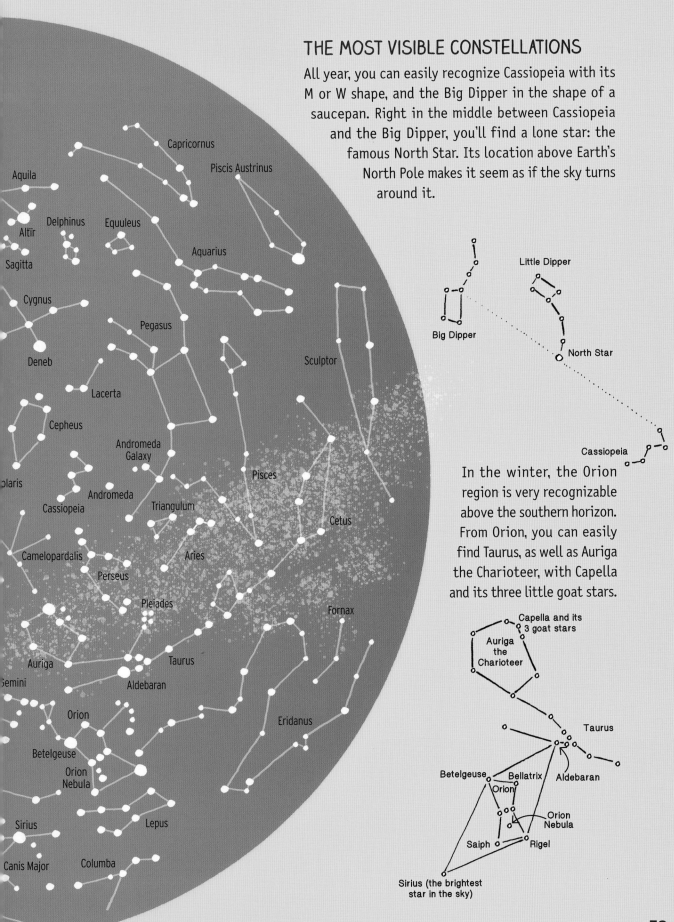

WHAT CAN YOU SEE IN THE

You can see more here than you can in the Northern Hemisphere.

Wow! So many stars!

CRUX, OR THE SOUTHERN CROSS

An icon of the southern sky, this is the smallest of all constellations, but can be immediately recognized by its four bright stars arranged around a dimmer fifth one near the center. Crux has been used by navigators for centuries; the longer bar of the cross points toward the South Pole.

THE BRIGHTEST STAR

As in the Northern Hemisphere, the brightest star in the night sky is Sirius. It is actually a binary star: two stars that orbit each other. They're nearly nine light-years from Earth, which means that their light takes almost nine years to reach us!

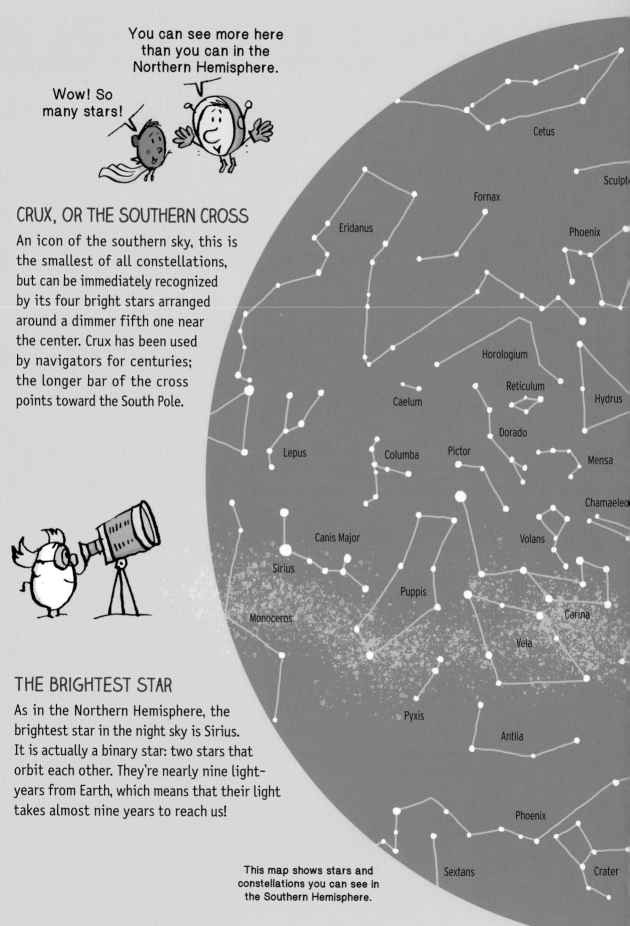

Cetus

Sculpt•

Fornax

Eridanus

Phoenix

Horologium

Reticulum

Hydrus

Caelum

Dorado

Mensa

Lepus

Columba

Pictor

Chamaeleo•

Volans

Canis Major

Sirius

Puppis

Carina

Monoceros

Vela

Pyxis

Antlia

Phoenix

Sextans

Crater

This map shows stars and constellations you can see in the Southern Hemisphere.

SOUTHERN NIGHT SKY?

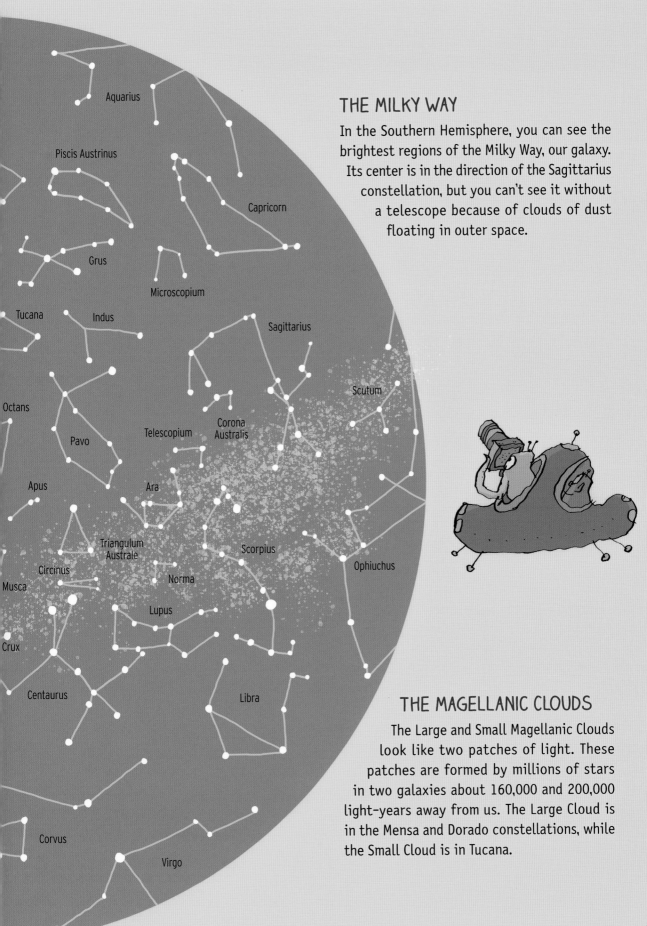

THE MILKY WAY

In the Southern Hemisphere, you can see the brightest regions of the Milky Way, our galaxy. Its center is in the direction of the Sagittarius constellation, but you can't see it without a telescope because of clouds of dust floating in outer space.

THE MAGELLANIC CLOUDS

The Large and Small Magellanic Clouds look like two patches of light. These patches are formed by millions of stars in two galaxies about 160,000 and 200,000 light-years away from us. The Large Cloud is in the Mensa and Dorado constellations, while the Small Cloud is in Tucana.

INDEX